MW00764821

# FIDGET SPINNER

## 50 AWESOME TRICKS

igloobooks

# CONTENTS

# INTRODUCTION

Join in the craze of the century and learn how to perform incredible tricks with your fidget spinner!

This book is packed with 50 amazing fidget spinner tricks ranging from basic techniques all the way to awesome show-stoppers. With handy step-by-step guides for every trick, and helpful photos, too, you'll be a fidget spinner expert in no time!

# FIDGET SPINNERS EXPLAINED

Fidget spinners come in all sorts of different shapes, designs, and even colors. In fact, some of the tricks shown later on work best when using different colored spinners. Before you get started, take a look below to get to know what each part of your fantastic fidget spinner does.

## BLADES

The rotating parts of the spinner. Make sure nothing is touching the blades so they can move freely.

## BLADE WEIGHTS

The weights ensure smooth rotation of the spinner.

## RAISED CAPS

These allow you to hold the spinner at the top and the bottom, so the blades can rotate freely.

# EASY TRICKS

# PINCH AND SPIN ①

## STEP 1

The very first thing you need to master! Hold the spinner in your right-hand (left if you're left-handed) by placing your index finger on the spinner's top cap and your thumb underneath its bottom cap.

## STEP 2

Use the index finger on your other hand to give one of the blades a quick flick, causing the spinner to rotate.

## TOP TIP

When you flick the blade it should be very firm but also as smooth as possible. This will make the spinner rotate both faster and far longer.

# ONE HAND FLICK ② 

## STEP 1

A skill you need to master for tricks where you hold a spinner in each hand. As before, hold the spinner in one hand by placing your index finger on the top cap and your thumb underneath its bottom cap.

## STEP 2

This time, flick one of the blades by using a finger on the same hand. Experiment to see if the best results come from using your middle, third, or pinky finger.

# BALANCING SPIN

**(3)**

## STEP 1

Start the spinner rotating in the usual way by holding it between index finger and thumb, and giving it a good flick with a finger on your other hand.

## STEP 2

When the spinner is rotating smoothly, gently lift your index finger from the top cap. The spinner should now be nicely balanced and rotating on your thumb!

## TOP TIP

A good way to perfect this trick is to time how long the spinner stays balanced and spinning on your thumb. The longer it spins, the more you have mastered the technique!

# DOUBLE SPIN

DIFFICULTY

## STEP 1

Hold the first spinner between the index finger and thumb of your left hand and give it a firm, smooth flick with a finger on your right hand to set it rotating.

## STEP 2

Place the second spinner between the index finger and thumb of your right hand. Then start rotating this spinner, too, with the flick of a finger on your right hand. Now carefully lift each index finger!

# DOUBLE STACK

**5**

## STEP 1

Stack two spinners between your index finger and thumb, holding firmly on the top cap of the first spinner and the bottom cap of the second spinner.

## STEP 2

First flick the bottom spinner to set it in motion. Now carefully flick the top spinner as well, making sure nothing is in the way to stop the rotation of the bottom spinner.

You might find it easier to flick both spinners together rather than one at a time. To do this, you must make sure that the blades of each spinner are perfectly lined up together before flicking them.

# TABLE STACK  DIFFICULTY

Stack the spinners on a flat surface, keeping the stack in place by pressing your finger on the top spinner's cap. Make sure all the blades are aligned and then give the blades a firm, smooth flick.

# TABLE STACK 2

## STEP 1

As in **Table Stack** (p.11), stack the spinners and press down on the top cap. But this time, do not align all the blades. This is so they can be flicked separately.

## STEP 2

Starting at the bottom of the stack, flick the bottom blade in a clockwise direction, the middle blade in a counterclockwise direction, and the top blade in a clockwise direction.

**TOP TIP**

This trick can create a lot of great patterns when the stack is viewed from above. Try changing the patterns by swapping some of the spinners for ones with a different color or shape.

# ELBOW SPIN

**8**

DIFFICULTY

Bend your right arm and raise your elbow until it is perfectly horizontal. Place a spinner on your elbow and press down on the top cap with your left index finger. Flick the blade with your thumb. Now try it with two spinners!

# KNEE SPIN

**9**

DIFFICULTY

Rotate the spinner on your knee. You can do this either sitting up with your knees in front of you or (a bit harder) lying on your back with your knees bent. Now try to keep a spinner revolving on each knee at the same time.

# THUMBS-UP SPIN

 **10**

## STEP 1

Some more on-the-body spins! Bend the top joint of your thumb upward, making it as vertical as possible. Place the spinner on top of your thumb and keep in place with your index finger.

## STEP 2

Flick one of the spinner's blades so that it rotates smoothly and then lift your index finger, holding the spinner well out of the way. Now very carefully straighten your thumb until it is fully vertical.

## TOP TIP

If you find this difficult, try it on your other hand. This is one of those tricks where the hand you use can make a surprising difference.

# KNUCKLE SPIN

**DIFFICULTY** 🌀

Make one of your hands into a fist. Hold the spinner on top of your index finger knuckle with the index finger of your other hand. Use the thumb of that other hand to set the spinner in motion and then carefully lift your index finger.

# BIG TOE SPIN

**DIFFICULTY** 🌀

With your big toe as vertical as possible, place the spinner carefully on the tip. Use a finger to hold the spinner in place until you've got it nicely rotating and balanced, then carefully lift your finger.

# MAGIC SPINNER

 13

## STEP 1

This one's a bit of a cheat, but an absolute show-stopper! Secretly put a piece of double-sided sticky tape on the spinner's top cap. Then hold the spinner between your index finger and thumb, ready for your show.

## STEP 2

Flick the spinner to set it in motion. Normally, you would now lift your index finger from the top, but this time you lower your thumb from the bottom. To everyone's amazement, the revolving spinner seems to be flying in the air!

# 2X MAGIC SPINNER

**14** DIFFICULTY

This trick is very similar to **Magic Spinner** (p.16) only instead of using one spinner, you double the magic by using two. As before, place double-sided sticky tape on the top caps of both spinners. Holding one of the spinners in your left hand, and the other in your right, start both spinners rotating. Then, remove both of your thumbs to see both spinners floating in the air!

**TOP TIP**

There are lots of different variations to this trick you might like to try, such as placing the spinners on a hard surface and lifting them off the ground like a pair of helicopters.

# DIE TOP SPIN

**DIFFICULTY**

## STEP 1

Try this game of chance! Place a die on a firm surface and a spinner on top of the die. Press a finger on the top cap of the spinner and give one of the blades a firm, smooth flick. Carefully lift your finger.

## STEP 2

If you would like to make this trick more challenging, place a stack of spinners on top of the die.

## TOP TIP

For an even tougher challenge, use the smallest die you can find!

# BOTTLE TOP SPIN 16

DIFFICULTY

Place the spinner on the cap of a plastic bottle and hold with your left index finger. Flick one of the blades firmly and smoothly with your right index finger, then lift your left index finger. If you find this too easy, try a stack of spinners.

# PENCIL TOP SPIN 17

DIFFICULTY

Make sure you use a pencil with a flat top. Use your index finger to press a spinner to the end of a pencil. Start spinning, then lift your index finger. This trick is easier if you keep the pointed end of the pencil pressed against a firm surface.

# PAIR OF SPINNERS (18)

## STEP 1

Grip the first spinner between the index finger and thumb of your left hand. Grip the second spinner between the index finger and thumb of your right hand.

## STEP 2

Remind yourself of the **One Hand Flick** (p.7), where you learned how to rotate a spinner using a finger on the same hand that gripped it. Do this for both spinners.

## TOP TIP

As before, experiment to see which finger on the same hand that you're holding the spinner with gives you the fastest and smoothest flick. It might be a different finger for each hand!

# SKILLED TRICKS

# HAND PASS

**DIFFICULTY**

## STEP 1

Hold a spinner vertically between the index finger and thumb of your left hand. Start to rotate with a firm, smooth flick.

## STEP 2

While the spinner is still rotating, "jump" it across to the index finger and thumb of your right hand. Make sure your fingers catch the spinner right in the center, avoiding the blades.

## TOP TIP

For your first few attempts, try "jumping" the spinner across just a few inches to perfect your technique. Then gradually move your hands further apart.

# AIR JUMP

As with the **Hand Pass** (p.22), you again "jump" the spinner from one hand to the other, but this time your first hand tosses it upward slightly into the air. Again, it's essential that you catch the spinner in the center to keep it rotating.

# SAME HAND JUMP **21**

Rotate the spinner vertically between the index finger and thumb of your right hand. Toss it slightly into the air and catch it between the index finger and thumb of the same hand. Remember to catch it in the center to avoid the blades.

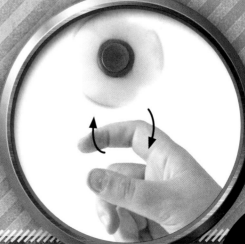

# VERTICAL PASS

**DIFFICULTY**

## STEP 1

Have a friend stand opposite you, ready with their index finger and thumb wide enough apart to catch the spinner.

## STEP 2

Rotate the spinner vertically between your index finger and thumb and then "jump" it carefully to your friend's wide-open index finger and thumb. Your throw needs to be as accurate as possible.

## TOP TIP

This trick requires perfect timing from both of you. Try taking turns, so your friend is the thrower and you're the catcher.

Your friend's index finger and thumb need to catch the spinner exactly in the center, avoiding the blades. This means the spinner should have continued rotating all the way from your hand to theirs.

# HORIZONTAL PASS 23

**DIFFICULTY**

Hold the spinner horizontally between your index finger and thumb, while your friend also holds their index finger and thumb horizontally. As before, "jump" the spinner to your friend's fingers. They must try to catch the spinner in its center, avoiding the blades.

# FOREARM CATCH

**DIFFICULTY**

## STEP 1

Rotate the spinner vertically between the index finger and thumb of your left hand. Hold your right arm in front of you, with your elbow bent, so that your forearm is at an angle.

## STEP 2

Pass the spinner under your right forearm and toss it upward. Catch the spinner, still vertical and spinning, in your right hand.

**TOP TIP**

With catching tricks, it helps to bend your knees slightly as you catch.

# OVER LEG JUMP  25

Sit on a chair with your right heel resting on another chair so that your leg is outstretched. Place your left arm to the left of your leg. Rotate the spinner in your right hand, then hold it vertically below the right side of your leg, toss it over your leg, and catch with your left hand.

# OVER LEG JUMP 2 26

DIFFICULTY

As with **Over Leg Jump** (p.27), carefully toss the spinner over your leg from below its right side. Now, quickly pass that throwing hand under your leg to catch the spinner, still rotating, below your leg's left side.

# DROP CATCH

DIFFICULTY

## STEP 1

Hold your left hand a little above your right hand. Grasp the spinner between the index finger and thumb of your left hand and flick it to give it a smooth rotation.

## STEP 2

Release the spinner from your left hand so that it drops down toward your right hand, which is placed slightly below it.

As the dropped spinner approaches your right hand, catch it carefully by the central caps so that you avoid the blades. This will keep the spinner rotating after it has been caught.

# LIFT CATCH

**28**

## DIFFICULTY

This is **Drop Catch** (p.28-29) in reverse. Hold the spinner in your right hand and give it a good, smooth flick with the index finger of your left hand. Now raise your left hand a little above your right hand and toss the spinner up toward it. Catch the spinner by the two central caps.

DIFFICULTY

## STEP 1

Hold the spinner horizontally between the index finger and thumb of your right hand. Flick it with another finger on that hand or, if you find it easier, the index finger of your left hand.

## STEP 2

Raise your right knee slightly and let the spinner fall horizontally on to it. As it falls, flick your knee so that the spinner bounces up toward your hand, and catch it neatly by the two central caps.

# 2X KNEE BOUNCE

**DIFFICULTY**

## STEP 1

You can do a **2x Knee Bounce** in two ways. First, drop the spinner on to your knee and bounce it twice before flicking it up to catch it.

## STEP 2

Second, bounce the spinner from your knee up to your hand once. Then, with it still neatly spinning, drop it on to your knee again and bounce it back to your hand a second time.

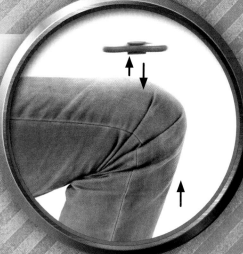

**TOP TIP**

Remember, don't try to do skilled tricks too quickly. A smooth, controlled technique usually produces better results.

# HAND TWIST

**DIFFICULTY**
♣ ♣ ♣ ♣

## STEP 1

Hold the spinner horizontally, with your index finger on the central cap at the top and your thumb on the cap at the bottom. Flick the spinner firmly to give it a fast, smooth spin.

## STEP 2

Lifting your index finger right out of the way, use your thumb to toss the spinner upward. As the spinner comes back down again, quickly turn your hand over so that you catch it, with your thumb now at the top of the spinner, and your index finger at the bottom.

# OVER THE ARM

**32**

## STEP 1

Rotate the spinner horizontally between the index finger and thumb of your right hand.

## STEP 2

Holding your left forearm stationary above it, toss the spinner upward so that it loops over your forearm and comes down on the other side for you to catch it.

**TOP TIP**

Some people find this trick easier if the spinner is tossed and caught vertically instead. Practice to see which works best for you.

# AROUND THE LEG

## STEP 1

Hold the spinner horizontally in your left hand, raise your left knee, and pass the spinner under the knee before releasing it upward.

## STEP 2

Catch the spinner neatly in your right hand, careful to avoid the blades, so you can keep it rotating.

**TOP TIP**

When throwing with one hand and catching with the other, use your strongest hand to do the catching.

# AROUND AGAIN

DIFFICULTY

Repeat **Around the Leg** (p.34), but when you catch the spinner in your right hand, raise your right leg so that you can go immediately in the other direction. Pass the spinner under your right knee, release it upward, and this time catch it in your left hand.

# COMBO AROUND LEG **35**

DIFFICULTY

A "combo" is when you follow one spinner trick immediately with another. After completing an **Around the Leg** (p.34), do a **Hand Pass** (p.22), so that you return the spinner to the hand it started in.

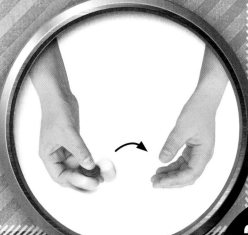

# BACKHAND BOUNCE

**DIFFICULTY**

## STEP 1

Rotate the spinner as fast as you can. Toss it slightly into the air and let it land on the back of the fingers of one hand. Immediately bounce the spinner upward again so that it crosses to the back of the fingers of the other hand.

## STEP 2

Keep quickly bouncing the spinner from the back of one hand across to the other, before flicking the spinner right up and neatly catching it.

## TOP TIP

For this trick to work well, the backs of your fingers need to be held as flat as possible.

# EXPERT TRICKS

**DIFFICULTY**
♣ ♣ ♣ ♣ ♣

## STEP 1

Hold your hand horizontally with your thumb at the top. Grip the spinner between your thumb and index finger and start it rotating. Lift your thumb to leave the spinner nicely balanced on the tip of your index finger.

## STEP 2

Gently flick the spinner upward a little, and catch it on your middle finger. Then flick it again and catch it on your third finger, then pinky finger.

## TOP TIP

Practice for this trick by making the spinner jump from your index finger to middle finger. Then, move on to the other fingers. When you have mastered each separate jump, you're ready to perform the trick!

# 2X FINGER JUMP

**DIFFICULTY**
♠ ♠ ♠ ♠ ♠

## STEP 1

As before, hold the spinner between your thumb and index finger, then lift your thumb to leave the spinner nicely balanced. Repeatedly hop the spinner gently upward a little so it jumps from one finger to the next.

## STEP 2

When the spinner has reached your pinky finger, gently flick it upward, catching it on the tip of your index finger. Then, make it jump again from one finger to another down to your pinky finger, finishing with a jump back to your index finger.

# FINGER TWIST

**DIFFICULTY**

## STEP 1

With the palm of your hand facing upward, straighten your index finger and balance the spinner on top. Keep it stable with your thumb on the upper cap until the spinner is rotating.

## STEP 2

Twisting your wrist backward and forward, move your finger in all sorts of directions—sometimes bent, sometimes half bent—while keeping the spinner constantly balanced and rotating.

# BACKHAND JUMP ④⓪

With your palm facing upward, place the spinner on your index finger and rotate. Gently toss the spinner into the air. At the same time, quickly turn your hand and bend your index finger so that you catch the spinner on the second joint of your finger.

# BACKHAND JUMP 2 ④①

Proceed as above until the spinner is rotating on the second joint of your bent index finger. Gently toss the spinner a little into the air, at the same time quickly turning your hand so you can catch the spinner on the tip of your middle finger.

## STEP 1

Hold the first spinner horizontally between your left hand's index finger and thumb, and the second spinner horizontally between your right hand's index finger and thumb.

## STEP 2

Set each spinner in motion. You can do this either by using a finger on the same hand, or a free finger from the other hand. Choose the technique that gives you the fastest rotation for each spinner.

## TOP TIP

So that the spinners don't collide during the swap over, make sure you arc one of the spinners clearly over the top of the other one.

With your hands at the same level and about 8 in (20 cm) apart, gently toss each spinner to the other hand at the same time, catching them while they are still rotating.

# AROUND THE BACK **43** DIFFICULTY

Hold the spinner vertically between the index finger and thumb of your left hand. Set the spinner rotating fast, then toss it up and behind your back so that it passes over your right shoulder. Catch the spinner, still rotating, in between the index finger and thumb of your right hand.

# JUGGLE SPIN

## DIFFICULTY

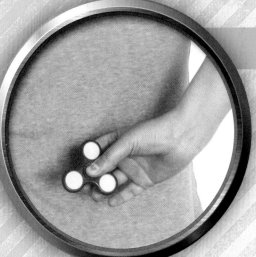

## STEP 1

Rotate the spinner horizontally in your left hand. Start with **Around the Back** (p.43), tossing the spinner behind your back and catching it, still rotating, in your hand.

## STEP 2

Immediately follow up with an **Around the Leg** (p.34), then a **Knee Bounce** (p.30) on your right knee and one on your left. Finally, catch the spinner between your index finger and thumb, with it still rotating smoothly.

## TOP TIP

For long or combo tricks, you need to have the spinner rotating as fast as possible, or it will not last until the end of the trick!

# SUPER JUGGLE SPIN (45) DIFFICULTY ♟♟♟♟♟

Rotate the spinner between index finger and thumb, toss it into the air, and balance it, still rotating fast, on the tip of an upright finger. After an **Around the Leg** (p.34), catch and balance the spinner on your fingertip, and again after a **Knee Bounce** (p.30).

# FINGERTIP PASS (46) DIFFICULTY ♟♟♟♟♟

Rotate the spinner horizontally between the index finger and thumb of your right hand. Toss the spinner across to your left hand and catch it by balancing it on a fingertip. Toss the spinner back to your right hand, and again, catch it on a fingertip.

# DROP AND LIFT

DIFFICULTY

## STEP 1

Hold the spinner horizontally between your index finger and thumb and flick to rotate. Drop the spinner a little, and at the same time, twist your hand so that you can catch it balanced on a fingertip.

## STEP 2

Now toss the spinner upward from your fingertip, turning your hand so that you can grasp it between your index finger and thumb again. Switching from hand to hand between drops and lifts makes this trick even more awesome!

# BLADE-HOLD SPIN (48)

Hold the spinner vertically with your index finger and thumb, pinching the middle of one of its blades. Throw the spinner upward to set it rotating and catch it neatly by the central caps—or balance it on a fingertip if you really want to show off!

# SUPER SPIN (49)

Balance the rotating spinner on your right index finger and toss it high into the air so that it's well above your head. Before the spinner comes down again, quickly spin around in a full circle and catch the spinner with the same finger.

# SUPER JUMP

**50**

## STEP 1

Hold the spinner horizontally between your index finger and thumb and start it rotating. Pull your index finger out of the way and toss the spinner slightly into the air. At the same time, raise your hand vertically so that you can catch the spinner on the top of your index finger.

## STEP 2

When you're sure you have the spinner nicely balanced, toss it gently across to the top of the next finger. Continue right down to the top of your pinky finger.

**TOP TIP**

A difficult trick like this requires amazing precision, so relax and don't rush. This is the secret behind all the expert spinner tricks.